NEW YEAR

TRADITIONS AROUND THE WORLD

BY ANN MALASPINA · ILLUSTRATED BY ELISA CHAVARRI

The Child's World®
childsworld.com

Published by The Child's World®
1980 Lookout Drive • Mankato, MN 56003-1705
800-599-READ • www.childsworld.com

PHOTOS
Cover: NIKS ADS/Shutterstock.com
Interior: cate_89/Shutterstock.com, 5; artapartment/
Shutterstock.com, 9; Marie1969/Shutterstock.com, 13;
Scharfsinn/Shutterstock.com, 15; David Cohen 156/
Shutterstock.com, 19; phive/Shutterstock.com, 21; windmoon/
Shutterstock.com, 24; wong yu liang/Shutterstock.com, 29;
Master the moment/Shutterstock.com, 30

ISBN 9781503850187 (Reinforced Library Binding)
ISBN 9781503851085 (Portable Document Format)
ISBN 9781503851849 (Online Multi-user eBook)
LCCN 2021930076

Printed in the United States of America

ABOUT THE AUTHOR

Ann Malaspina is the author of many books for children. When she was growing up, her mother baked Vasilopita on New Year's Eve. Her father cut the Greek sweet bread at midnight. Ann always hoped she, and not her brothers, would get the lucky coin.

ABOUT THE ILLUSTRATOR

Elisa Chavarri is a Peruvian illustrator who works from her home in northern Michigan. She loves to create artwork that inspires curiosity and happiness in people of all ages.

TABLE OF CONTENTS

CHAPTER ONE

HAPPY NEW YEAR!

Fireworks light up the sky at midnight on December 31. The New Year's Eve ball drops in Times Square in New York City. It is now 12:01 a.m. on January 1. People hug their friends and family. They wish each other a happy new year. Bands play and everyone dances.

In ancient times, some people celebrated New Year's Day in the spring. Others celebrated at harvest time in the fall. In 153 BC, the Romans made a new calendar. January 1 became the first day of the year.

Many cultures still follow ancient calendars for holidays. Chinese New Year, or Spring Festival, starts in the first month of the Chinese calendar. This is in late January or early February. Jews and Muslims celebrate their New Year holidays at different times in the fall. In Thailand, New Year is in April. The New Year is a religious holiday for many people.

Fireworks always light the sky in New York City to celebrate the New Year.

People do many things for luck on New Year's Day. People go to the beach in Brazil. They jump over seven waves and make seven wishes for the coming year. In Scotland, the first visitor of the New Year is called the "first footer." It is good luck if the first footer is a man with dark hair.

The New Year is a time to put the past behind. The bells in the Buddhist temples in Japan toll at midnight on January 31. They toll 108 times to get rid of feelings such as jealousy and anger. When the bells stop, the New Year has begun.

The New Year is a time to start something new. People make resolutions. They decide to eat more vegetables, learn a new sport, or always wear a bike helmet. Some resolutions are hard to keep. You can always try again next year!

WATER FESTIVAL

*S*ongkran (SONG-kran) is the New Year festival in Thailand. It is in the spring. Children pour water on grandparents' hands. Families sprinkle sweet-smelling water on images of Buddha. In the streets, water sprays everywhere. Even elephants get wet. It is said the water cleans the soul for the New Year.

Songkran is a time to be generous. People give gifts. They bring food to the monks at the temple. Families eat a rice dish called *khao chae* (KAOW CHEH). The rice is cooked with flower blossoms. It tastes delicious!

Letting birds and fish go free is a favorite Songkran tradition. People also tie strings around their friends' wrists and say blessings. By the end of Songkran, people have many strings tied around their wrists!

People celebrate Songkran with a huge water fight in the streets.

CHAPTER THREE

FREEDOM SOUP

In Haiti, New Year's Day is also Independence Day. Haiti became independent from France on January 1, 1804. To honor the important event, Haitians eat pumpkin soup for breakfast on January 1. It's called Soup *Joumou* (ZHOO-moo). Joumou means "pumpkin" in Haitian Creole. Before independence, only French people and white people were allowed to eat soup. So former Black slaves celebrated independence by eating soup.

The soup is made from Caribbean pumpkin, beef, spaghetti, and lots of vegetables and spices. It is tasty and filling. After the last spoonful, people walk from house to house to wish their neighbors *"Bòn ane!"* (BON AH-nay), or Happy New Year!

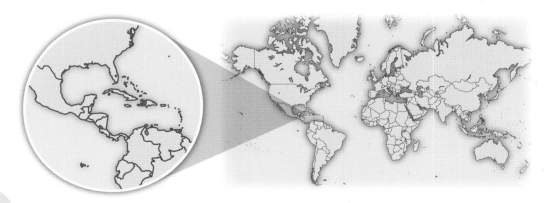

CHAPTER FOUR

COUNT DOWN TO THE NEW YEAR

At 11:59 p.m. on December 31, the New Year's Eve ball starts to drop in Times Square, New York. More than 1 billion people around the world watch on television. The ball falls at midnight. A ton of confetti rains down. Bands play the New Year song, "Auld Lang Syne." The New Year's Eve ball has dropped every year since 1907, except in 1942 and 1943 during World War II (1939–1945).

New Year's Day is a quiet day for family and friends. Pork is a lucky food for many families. Just as the New Year moves forward, pigs move forward when they dig with their noses. In the South, people eat ham with greens, rice, and black-eyed peas for a good year.

It is a big day for football in the United States. The Rose Bowl is the college football game played on January 1 in Pasadena, California. Crowds watch the Rose Parade in the morning. If January 1 is on Sunday, the game is played January 2. Other college football games are also played on January 1 or 2. Families watch the games on television and cheer for their favorite teams.

Floats in the Rose Parade are made of millions of flowers.

CHAPTER FIVE

FELIZ AÑO NUEVO

On New Year's Eve in Mexico, people pop firecrackers. Children break piñatas full of candy. Mariachi musicians play trumpets, violins, and guitars. A man in a wide hat called a sombrero sings to the crowds.

The traditional meal for New Year's Eve is *bacaloa* (bah-kah-LOH-ah). It is made with fish, tomatoes, potatoes, and olives. Families eat sweet fritters called *buñuelos* (boon-WAY-los) for dessert. Mexicans wear special colors on this day. Yellow brings good fortune. Red brings love in the coming year.

The church bells toll 12 times at midnight. Each person eats 12 grapes. As he or she swallows each grape, a wish is made for the New Year. Say *"¡Feliz Año Nuevo!"* (feh-LEES AN-yoh noo-WAY-voh), or Happy New Year!

Mariachi bands play on New Year's Eve in Mexico.

CHAPTER SIX

LUCKY COIN

January 1 is Saint Basil's Day in Greece. Saint Basil was a bishop who gave money to the poor. He slipped coins in the bread he gave away. People in Greece celebrate the New Year with a sweet bread. It's called *Vasilopita* (vah-see-LOH-pee-tah), or "sweet bread of Basil." The baker slips a coin into the Vasilopita.

Greeks stay up late on New Year's Eve. They play cards on this lucky night. They turn on the lights at midnight to welcome the year. Then the head of the family cuts the Vasilopita. There is a slice for Saint Basil and one for the house. Slices of the sweet bread are passed to everybody. The person who gets the coin will have a lucky year.

CHAPTER SEVEN

APPLES AND HONEY

Rosh Hashanah is the Jewish New Year. It is the first two days of the Jewish month of *Tishrei* (tish-RAY) in the fall. The two-day holiday is part of the ten days of *teshuvah* (teh-SHOO-vah), or repentance. Rosh Hashanah is celebrated in Israel, the Jewish homeland. It is celebrated around the world, too. Jews ask to be forgiven for mistakes. They plan to make changes in the coming year. Yom Kippur, the Day of Atonement, comes on the tenth day.

On Rosh Hashanah, people go to synagogue in the morning. The shofar is blown 100 times. The shofar is an ancient instrument made from a ram's horn. The shofar's blast tells people to think about how to make the world better in the next year.

Families gather for a meal at night. They dip challah in honey and say a blessing. Challah is a braided egg bread. On Rosh Hashanah, the challah is round for the circle of life. Jews also dip apple slices in honey. They ask God for a sweet year. Late on the second day, it is a tradition to toss bread into a river. The water carries away the bread. It gets rid of sins from the old year. Now the New Year begins.

The shofar is blown on Rosh Hashanah.

CHAPTER EIGHT

FESTIVAL OF LIGHTS

A new moon rises over India. Lanterns flicker in the windows. The lights guide *Lakshmi* (LAKSH-mee) into people's homes. Lakshmi is the Hindu goddess of spiritual and material wealth and beauty. Families wish Lakshmi will bring a prosperous new year.

Diwali (dee-VAH-lee), the Festival of Lights, is the New Year festival for Hindus. The holiday lasts for five days in the fall. Diwali celebrates the victory of light over darkness. People draw pictures called *rangoli* (ran-GO-lee) on their doorsteps in rice powder, limestone, or chalk. The pictures are birds, flowers, the sun, or geometric patterns. The beautiful pictures are meant to attract Lakshmi so she will bless the family.

The third day of Diwali is the Festival of Lights. Hindus line roofs, gardens, windows, and streets with clay lamps called *diyas* (DEE-yahs). The flames burn all night. India glows with hope and goodwill for the New Year.

People decorate for Diwali with rangoli designs and diya lamps.

CHAPTER NINE

DRAGON DANCING AND LUCKY RED ENVELOPES

Spring Festival welcomes the New Year in China. The important holiday is also known as Chinese New Year. It happens during the first month of the Chinese calendar. This is usually in January or February. It is a time for families and new beginnings.

Millions of Chinese travel many miles to their home villages. Families gather on the eve of the new moon for dinner together. Dumplings called *chiao-tzu* (JOW-zuh) symbolize prosperity. They are shaped like the money of ancient China. A whole fish is served. If people leave part of the fish, they will have extra food in the New Year.

On New Year's Day, children bow to adults. They wish their grandparents long lives. Children receive red envelopes with lucky money. Red is the lucky color for Spring Festival. People write wishes on red "lucky papers." Red firecrackers scare away evil spirits.

In the streets, people watch the Dragon Dance. Dragons mean wisdom, power, and wealth. Performers hold up dragons made of paper and cloth. The dragons weave through the crowds. Drums, gongs, and horns make lots of noise. The Dragon Dance brings good luck for the New Year.

Spring Festival ends with the Lantern Festival. Twinkling lanterns make a sea of lights. People eat rice dumplings that are as round as the full moon above. The Chinese believe this is a good night to fall in love.

Another year has begun. Every Chinese year is named after an animal. There are 12 animals, one for every year of the moon's cycle. Many believe that a person's character is like the animal of his or her birth year.

The Dragon Dance brings good luck for the next year.

CHAPTER TEN

NEW DAY

*N*owruz (NOH-rooz), the Persian New Year, is celebrated in Iran. Nowruz means "new day" in Persian, the language of Iran. The holiday falls on the first day of spring. It is a joyful time for families.

To get ready, Iranians plant *sabzeh* (SAB-zeh), or green sprouts. The sprouts breathe in the problems of the past year. A cloth with seven foods is laid out. Each food begins with the Persian letter *S. Seeb* (SEEB), or apples, are for beauty. *Serkeh* (SIR-keh), or vinegar, is for patience. Also on the table are oranges, colored eggs, goldfish, gold coins, and more. All symbolize good things for the New Year.

On the last Tuesday before the New Year, Iranians jump over a bonfire. The fire takes away bad things from the past year. When the sun passes over the equator, the New Year begins in Iran. This is around March 21. Families wish each other a happy new year. Children receive gifts, sweets, and nuts.

The 13th day of the year is called *Sizdah Bedar* (SIZ-dah BEE-dar). Families have a picnic. They throw the green sprouts into a river. The water takes away the past year. The New Year starts fresh.

UP CLOSE

The Story of Nian

Long ago in China, there was a terrible monster with sharp teeth. Every winter, at the end of the lunar year, he attacked the village. He ate the grain and tried to swallow the people. Everyone ran away to the mountains. They were so afraid of the monster called Nian.

One winter, a wise beggar walked into the village. He was not afraid of Nian. He refused to go to the mountains. An old grandmother let him stay in her house. She ran away to the mountains. Nian came again that night. This time, red paper hung from the grandmother's house. Candles lit up the house. When the angry beast ran at the house, noisy firecrackers exploded.

Nian shook with fear. He was afraid of the color red, light, and firecrackers. The wise beggar laughed at him. Nian fled into the darkness.

The villagers were happy when they heard what happened. They bought new clothes and congratulated each other. Never again would they fear the monster.

Every winter, at the end of the lunar year, the people hung up red paper scrolls. They lit lanterns and bonfires. Noisy firecrackers exploded, and Nian never returned. Today, Chinese people around the world celebrate the lunar New Year the same way. It is called Spring Festival, or Chinese New Year.

HANDS-ON

Diya Lanterns for Diwali

In India, Diwali celebrates light defeating darkness. Make a diya lantern to celebrate too!

Materials

- 1 cup (8 fl. oz.) water
- 2 cups (16 fl. oz.) white flour
- 2 cups (16 fl. oz.) salt
- paint brush
- paint (red, yellow, purple, or blue)
- sequins
- glue
- tea candle

Directions

1. To make salt dough, mix the water, flour, and salt. Form dough into balls. Use your thumbs to press down in middle. Make enough room for a tea candle in each ball.
2. Place dough on baking sheet. Bake at 250 degrees Fahrenheit (121°C) for two to three hours. A grown-up should do this step. Allow to cool.
3. Paint lanterns with pictures and designs. Use many colors or one color. Let dry. Glue sequins on painted lamp for decoration.
4. Place tea candles in lamps. Put the lamps in your window. Ask an adult to light the candles for you. Think about your blessings.

GLOSSARY

atonement (uh-TONE-munt) Atonement is a process someone undergoes to repair a broken relationship. A process of atonement can make up for doing something wrong.

celebrated (SEL-uh-bray-ted) If you have celebrated something, you have observed or taken notice of a special day. People celebrated the New Year at different times.

lanterns (LAN-turns) Lanterns are small decorative lights. People put out lanterns during Diwali.

prosperous (PRAHS-pur-us) Something prosperous is showing success. We wish you a prosperous New Year!

repentance (ri-PEN-tans) Repentance is feeling sorry for what you've done and deciding to do what's right. Jewish people feel repentance during their New Year celebrations.

resolutions (rez-uh-LOO-shuns) Resolutions are decisions. People make resolutions for the New Year.

synagogue (SIN-uh-gahg) A synagogue is a house of worship for Jews. People go to synagogue during Rosh Hashanah.

tradition (truh-DISH-un) A tradition is a way of thinking or acting communicated through culture. Watching the ball drop is a New Year tradition.

LEARN MORE

Books

Frankel, Valerie Estelle. *Chelm for the Holidays*.
Minneapolis, MN: Lerner, 2019.

Heinrichs, Ann. *Celebrating Chinese New Year*.
Mankato, MN: The Child's World, 2022.

Websites

Visit our website for links about New Year traditions
around the world: childsworld.com/links

*Note to Parents, Teachers, and Librarians: We routinely verify our Web links to make sure
they are safe and active sites. So encourage your readers to check them out!*

INDEX